My Ultimate Christmas Planner

This Planner Belongs to:

_____

_____

_____

Cellphone:

email id:

Contents

Also Included: My Scribbles
                   Notes for Next Year

Calendar

1st	2nd	3rd	4th	5th
6th	7th	8th	9th	10th
11th	12th	13th	14th	15th

November

16th	17th	18th	19th	20th
21st	22nd	23rd	24th	25th
26th	27th	28th	29th	30th

December

1st	2nd	3rd	4th	5th
6th	7th	8th	9th	10th
11th	12th	13th	14th	15th
				16th
17th	18th	19th	20th	21st
22nd	23rd	24th	25th	26th
27th	28th	29th	30th	31st

Weekly Planner

Monday

Tuesday

Wednesday

Thursday

Friday

Saturday

Sunday

TO DO

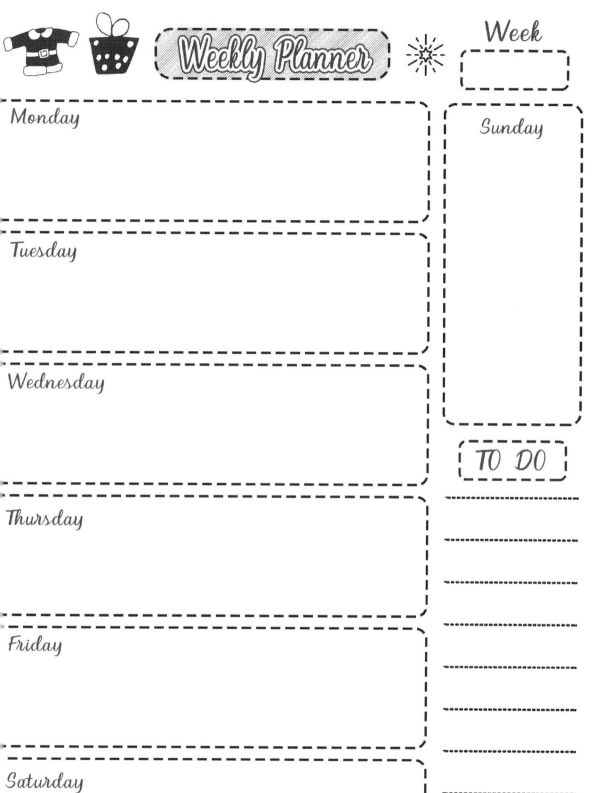

Weekly Planner

Week

Monday

Tuesday

Wednesday

Thursday

Friday

Saturday

Sunday

TO DO

Weekly Planner

Monday

Tuesday

Wednesday

Thursday

Friday

Saturday

Sunday

TO DO

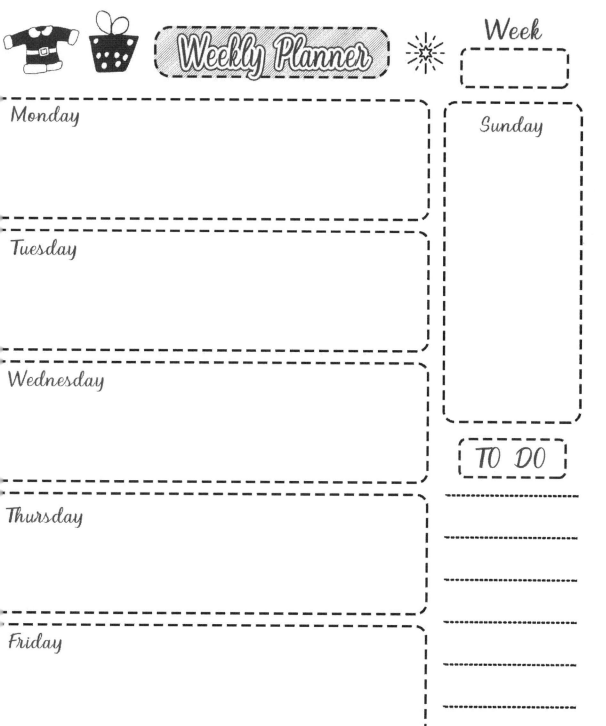

Weekly Planner

Week

Monday

Tuesday

Wednesday

Thursday

Friday

Saturday

Sunday

TO DO

Weekly Planner

Week

Monday

Tuesday

Wednesday

Thursday

Friday

Saturday

Sunday

TO DO

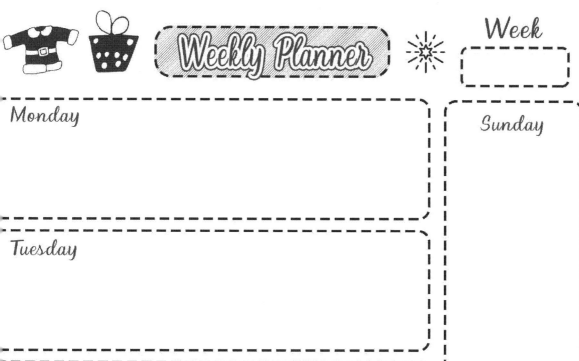

Weekly Planner

Week

Monday

Tuesday

Wednesday

Thursday

Friday

Saturday

Sunday

TO DO

Weekly Planner

Week

Monday

Tuesday

Wednesday

Thursday

Friday

Saturday

Sunday

TO DO

Weekly Planner

Week

Monday

Tuesday

Wednesday

Thursday

Friday

Saturday

Sunday

TO DO

My CHRISTMAS Goals

My Top 10 Plans

_____

1. _____
2. _____
3. _____
4. _____
5. _____
6. _____
7. _____
8. _____
9. _____
10. _____

Quick Wish List

 Home

_____

Family

_____

Guests

_____

Party

_____

Quick Wish List

Shopping

_____
_____
_____
_____

_____
_____
_____
_____

Decorations

_____
_____
_____

_____
_____
_____

Gift & Cards

_____
_____
_____

_____
_____
_____

Food

_____
_____
_____

_____
_____
_____

My Bucket list

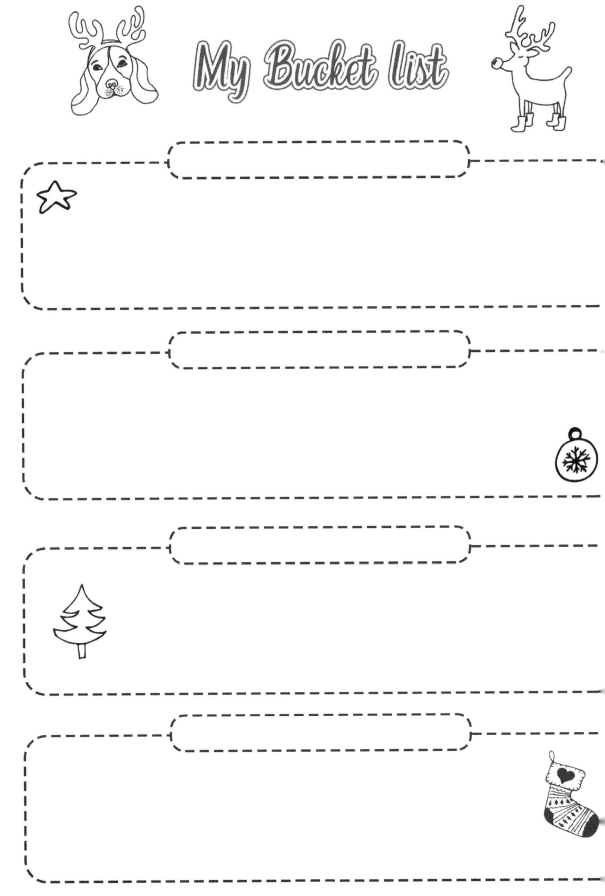

My Bucket list

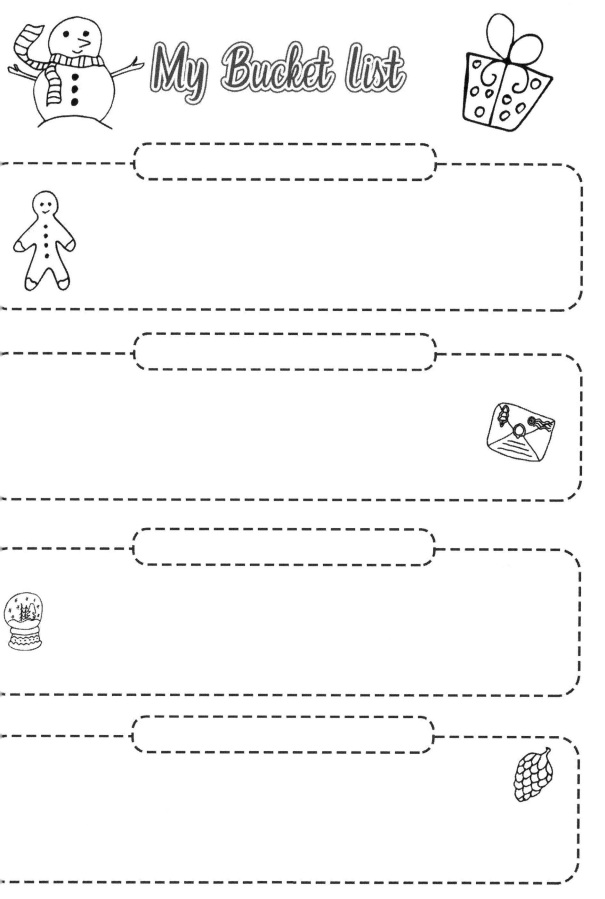

My Bucket list

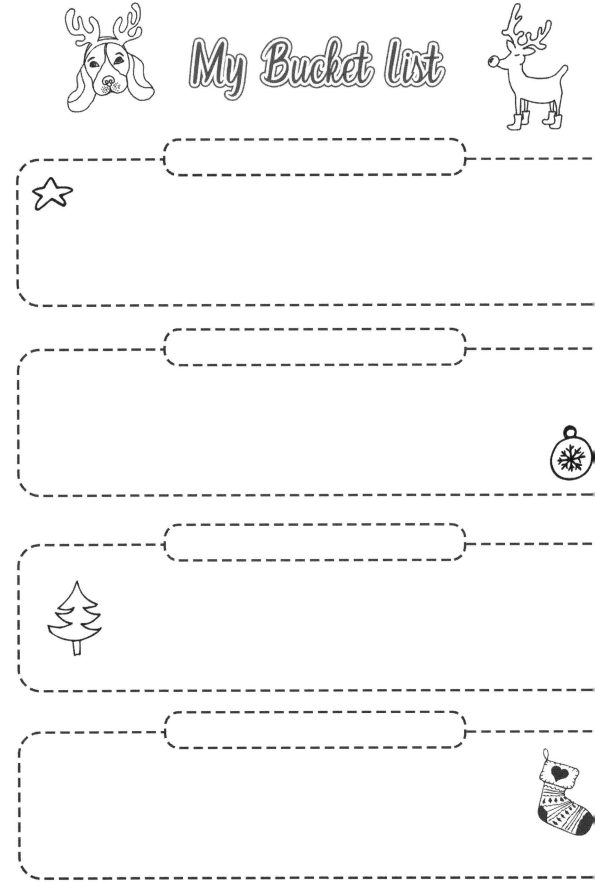

My Bucket list

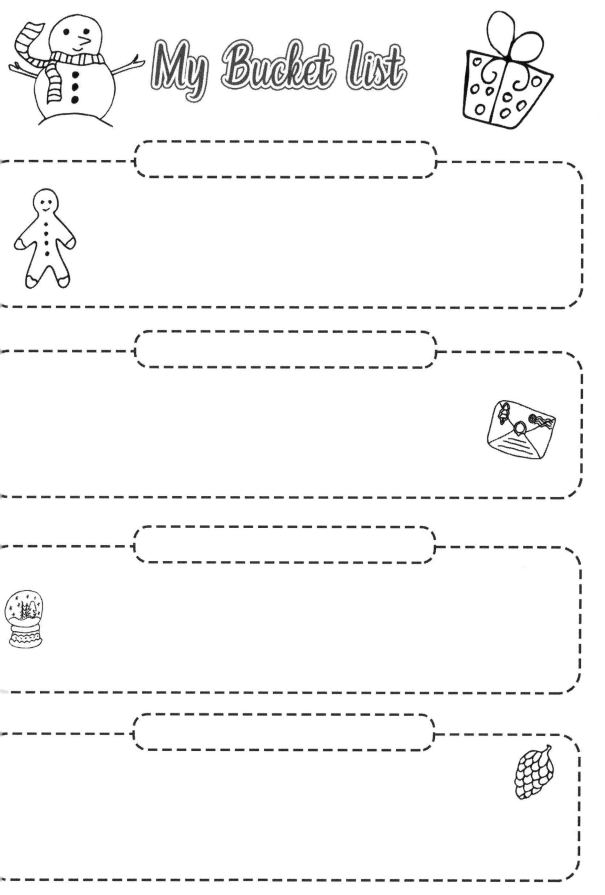

My Bucket list

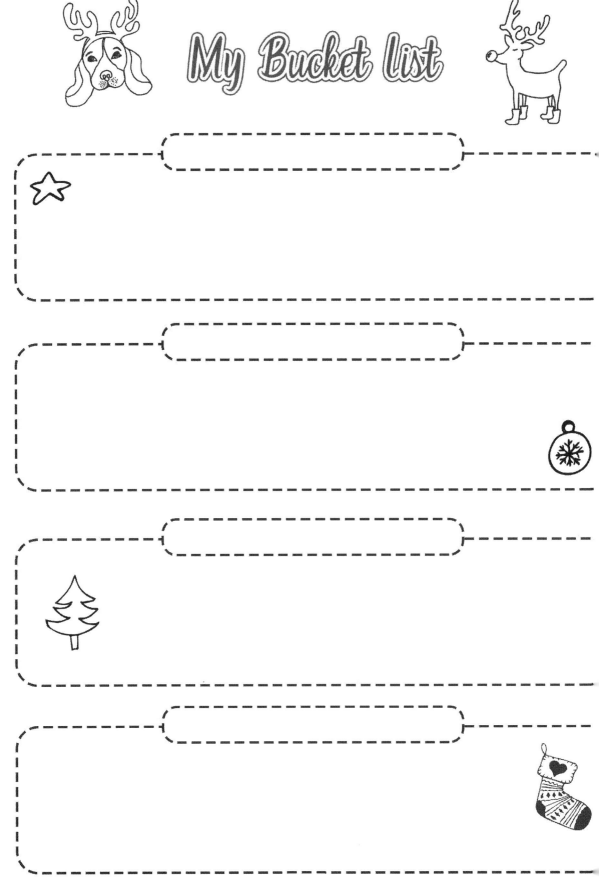

My Bucket list

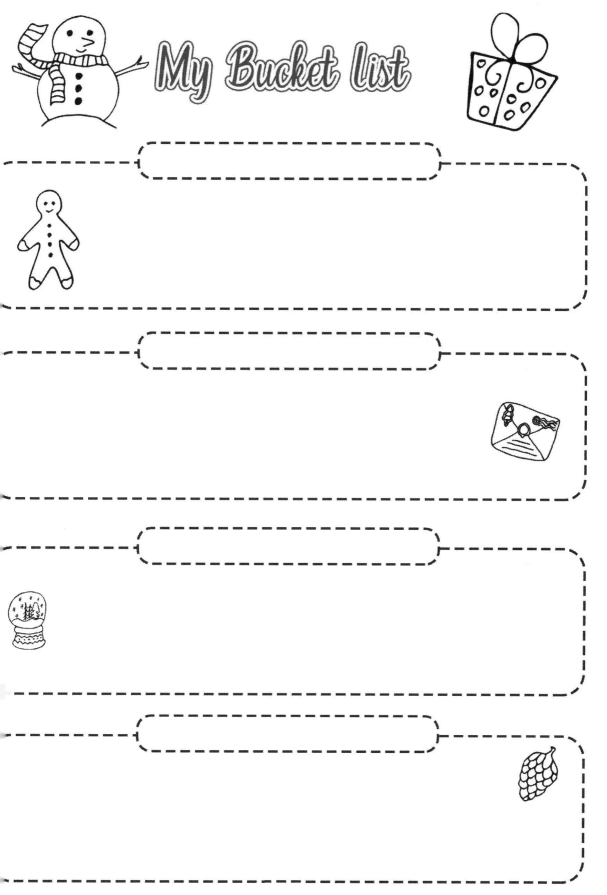

My Bucket list

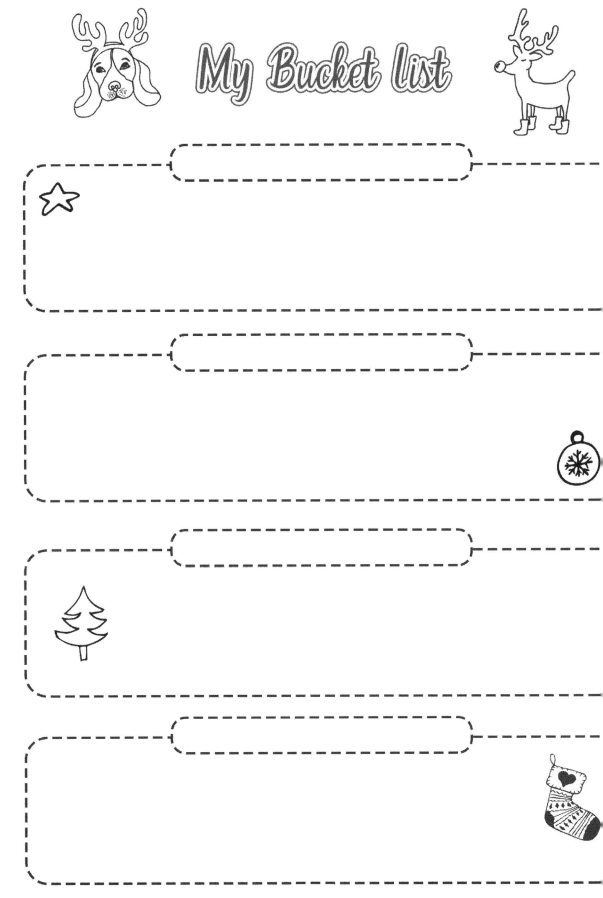

My Bucket list

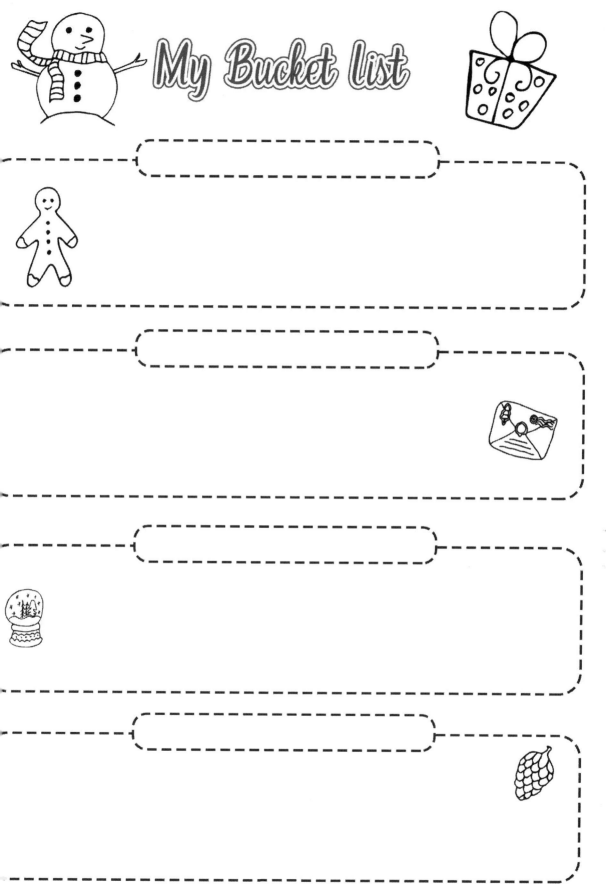

Countdown Checklist

November

Things to do:

1st Week

- [ ]
- [ ]
- [ ]
- [ ]
- [ ]
- [ ]
- [ ]

2nd Week

- [ ]
- [ ]
- [ ]
- [ ]
- [ ]
- [ ]
- [ ]

3rd Week

- [ ]
- [ ]
- [ ]
- [ ]
- [ ]
- [ ]
- [ ]

4th Week

- [ ]
- [ ]
- [ ]
- [ ]
- [ ]
- [ ]
- [ ]

Countdown Checklist

December

Things to do:

1st December

- ☐
- ☐
- ☐
- ☐
- ☐
- ☐
- ☐

2nd December

- ☐
- ☐
- ☐
- ☐
- ☐
- ☐
- ☐

3rd December

- ☐
- ☐
- ☐
- ☐
- ☐
- ☐
- ☐

4th December

- ☐
- ☐
- ☐
- ☐
- ☐
- ☐
- ☐

Countdown Checklist

December

Things to do:

5th December
- ☐
- ☐
- ☐
- ☐
- ☐
- ☐
- ☐

6th December
- ☐
- ☐
- ☐
- ☐
- ☐
- ☐
- ☐

7th December
- ☐
- ☐
- ☐
- ☐
- ☐
- ☐
- ☐

8th December
- ☐
- ☐
- ☐
- ☐
- ☐
- ☐
- ☐

Countdown Checklist

December

Things to do:

9th December

- ☐
- ☐
- ☐
- ☐
- ☐
- ☐
- ☐

10th December

- ☐
- ☐
- ☐
- ☐
- ☐
- ☐
- ☐

11th December

- ☐
- ☐
- ☐
- ☐
- ☐
- ☐
- ☐

12th December

- ☐
- ☐
- ☐
- ☐
- ☐
- ☐
- ☐

Countdown Checklist

December

Things to do:

13th December
- ☐
- ☐
- ☐
- ☐
- ☐
- ☐
- ☐

14th December
- ☐
- ☐
- ☐
- ☐
- ☐
- ☐
- ☐

15th December
- ☐
- ☐
- ☐
- ☐
- ☐
- ☐
- ☐

16th December
- ☐
- ☐
- ☐
- ☐
- ☐
- ☐
- ☐

Countdown Checklist

December

Things to do:

17th December

18th December

19th December

20th December

Countdown Checklist

December

Things to do:

21st December

- [ ]
- [ ]
- [ ]
- [ ]
- [ ]
- [ ]
- [ ]

22nd December

- [ ]
- [ ]
- [ ]
- [ ]
- [ ]
- [ ]
- [ ]

23rd December

- [ ]
- [ ]
- [ ]
- [ ]
- [ ]
- [ ]
- [ ]

24th December

- [ ]
- [ ]
- [ ]
- [ ]
- [ ]
- [ ]
- [ ]

Merry Christmas

Things to do:

25th December

Master Holiday Budget

No.	Category	Budget	Actual
	⭐ Grand Total		

Budget Planner

Category: _____

No.	Item	Budget	Actual
	🎄 Total		

Budget Planner

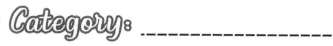

Category: _____

No.	Item	Budget	Actual
	Total		

Budget Planner

 **Category:** _____

No.	Item	Budget	Actual
	🎄 Total		

Budget Planner

Category: _____

No.	Item	Budget	Actual
	Total		

Budget Planner

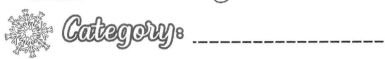 **Category:** _____

No.	Item	Budget	Actual
	🎄 Total		

Budget Planner

 Category: _____

No.	Item	Budget	Actual
	Total		

Budget Planner

 Category: _____

No.	Item	Budget	Actual
	Total		

Budget Planner

Category: _____

No.	Item	Budget	Actual
	🎄 Total		

Holiday Traditions

Tradition :   Date:

Tradition :   Date:

Tradition :   Date:

 # Holiday Traditions

Tradition :   Date:

Tradition :   Date:

Tradition :   Date:

Holiday Traditions

Tradition :   Date:

Tradition :   Date:

Tradition :   Date:

 # Holiday Traditions

Tradition :   Date:

Tradition :   Date:

Tradition :   Date:

Holiday Traditions

Tradition :   Date:

Tradition :   Date:

Tradition :   Date:

 # Holiday Traditions

Tradition :   Date:

Tradition :   Date:

Tradition :   Date:

Movies to watch this Holiday

Movie Names   **Seen**

TV Shows & Web Series List

Show Names

Seen

 # My Outdoor Ideas

No.	Location	Event	Done
			☐
			☐
			☐
			☐
			☐
			☐
			☐
			☐
			☐
			☐
			☐
			☐
			☐

My Indoor Activity Ideas

No.	Activity	Supplies	Done
			☐
			☐
			☐
			☐
			☐
			☐
			☐

 # My Outdoor Ideas

No.	Location	Event	Done
			☐
			☐
			☐
			☐
			☐
			☐
			☐
			☐
			☐
			☐
			☐
			☐
			☐
			☐

My Indoor Activity Ideas

No.	Activity	Supplies	Done
			☐
			☐
			☐
			☐
			☐
			☐
			☐

My Elf Month Antics

1st	
2nd	
3rd	
4th	
5th	
6th	
7th	
8th	
9th	
10th	
11th	
12th	
13th	
14th	
15th	
16th	
17th	
18th	
19th	
20th	
21st	
22nd	
23rd	
24th	

My Elf Supplies

- _____ ◻
- _____ ◻
- _____ ◻
- _____ ◻
- _____ ◻
- _____ ◻
- _____ ◻
- _____ ◻
- _____ ◻
- _____ ◻

- _____ ◻
- _____ ◻
- _____ ◻
- _____ ◻
- _____ ◻
- _____ ◻
- _____ ◻
- _____ ◻
- _____ ◻
- _____ ◻

My Elf Name

My Elf Notes

Cards and Gifts

 # My Card List

Name	Address	Sent

 # My Card List

Name	Address	Sent

 # My Card List

Name	Address	Sent

My Card List

Name	Address	Sent

My Card List

Name	Address	Sent

My Card List

Name	Address	Sent

 # My Card List

Name	Address	Sent

My Card List

Name	Address	Sent

 # My Card list

Name	Address	Sent

 # Gift Ideas

Recipient Name: _____

Address: _____

_____

Gift Ideas:

Recipient Name: _____

Address: _____

_____

Gift Ideas:

Recipient Name: _____

Address: _____

_____

Gift Ideas:

Recipient Name: _____

Address: _____

_____

Gift Ideas:

Recipient Name: _____

Address: _____

_____

Gift Ideas:

Recipient Name: _____

Address: _____

_____

Gift Ideas:

 # Gift Ideas

Recipient Name: _____

Address: _____
_____

Gift Ideas:

Recipient Name: _____

Address: _____
_____

Gift Ideas:

Recipient Name: _____

Address: _____
_____

Gift Ideas:

Recipient Name: _____

Address: _____
_____

Gift Ideas:

Recipient Name: _____

Address: _____
_____

Gift Ideas:

Recipient Name: _____

Address: _____
_____

Gift Ideas:

 # Gift Ideas

Recipient Name: _____

Address: _____

_____

Gift Ideas:

Recipient Name: _____

Address: _____

_____

Gift Ideas:

Recipient Name: _____

Address: _____

_____

Gift Ideas:

Recipient Name: _____

Address: _____

_____

Gift Ideas:

Recipient Name: _____

Address: _____

_____

Gift Ideas:

Recipient Name: _____

Address: _____

_____

Gift Ideas:

 # Gift Ideas

Recipient Name: _____
Address: _____
_____
Gift Ideas:

Recipient Name: _____
Address: _____
_____
Gift Ideas:

Recipient Name: _____
Address: _____
_____
Gift Ideas:

Recipient Name: _____
Address: _____
_____
Gift Ideas:

Recipient Name: _____
Address: _____
_____
Gift Ideas:

Recipient Name: _____
Address: _____
_____
Gift Ideas:

 # Gift Ideas

Recipient Name: _____

Address: _____

_____

Gift Ideas:

Recipient Name: _____

Address: _____

_____

Gift Ideas:

Recipient Name: _____

Address: _____

_____

Gift Ideas:

Recipient Name: _____

Address: _____

_____

Gift Ideas:

Recipient Name: _____

Address: _____

_____

Gift Ideas:

Recipient Name: _____

Address: _____

_____

Gift Ideas:

 # Gift Ideas

Recipient Name: _____

Address: _____

_____

Gift Ideas:

Recipient Name: _____

Address: _____

_____

Gift Ideas:

Recipient Name: _____

Address: _____

_____

Gift Ideas:

Recipient Name: _____

Address: _____

_____

Gift Ideas:

Recipient Name: _____

Address: _____

_____

Gift Ideas:

Recipient Name: _____

Address: _____

_____

Gift Ideas:

 # Gift Ideas

Recipient Name: _____

Address: _____

_____

Gift Ideas:

Recipient Name: _____

Address: _____

_____

Gift Ideas:

Recipient Name: _____

Address: _____

_____

Gift Ideas:

Recipient Name: _____

Address: _____

_____

Gift Ideas:

Recipient Name: _____

Address: _____

_____

Gift Ideas:

Recipient Name: _____

Address: _____

_____

Gift Ideas:

 # Gift Ideas

Recipient Name: _____

Address: _____

_____

Gift Ideas:

Recipient Name: _____

Address: _____

_____

Gift Ideas:

Recipient Name: _____

Address: _____

_____

Gift Ideas:

Recipient Name: _____

Address: _____

_____

Gift Ideas:

Recipient Name: _____

Address: _____

_____

Gift Ideas:

Recipient Name: _____

Address: _____

_____

Gift Ideas:

 # Gift Ideas

Recipient Name: _____

Address: _____

_____

Gift Ideas:

Recipient Name: _____

Address: _____

_____

Gift Ideas:

Recipient Name: _____

Address: _____

_____

Gift Ideas:

Recipient Name: _____

Address: _____

_____

Gift Ideas:

Recipient Name: _____

Address: _____

_____

Gift Ideas:

Recipient Name: _____

Address: _____

_____

Gift Ideas:

 # Gift Ideas

Recipient Name: _____

Address: _____

_____

Gift Ideas:

Recipient Name: _____

Address: _____

_____

Gift Ideas:

Recipient Name: _____

Address: _____

_____

Gift Ideas:

Recipient Name: _____

Address: _____

_____

Gift Ideas:

Recipient Name: _____

Address: _____

_____

Gift Ideas:

Recipient Name: _____

Address: _____

_____

Gift Ideas:

Gift Tracker

Recipient Name	O	R	W	D
	☐	☐	☐	☐
	☐	☐	☐	☐
	☐	☐	☐	☐
	☐	☐	☐	☐
	☐	☐	☐	☐
	☐	☐	☐	☐
	☐	☐	☐	☐
	☐	☐	☐	☐
	☐	☐	☐	☐
	☐	☐	☐	☐
	☐	☐	☐	☐

O – Ordered   R – Received
W – Wrapped   D – Delivered

Gift Tracker

Recipient Name

	O	R	W	D
	☐	☐	☐	☐
	☐	☐	☐	☐
	☐	☐	☐	☐
	☐	☐	☐	☐
	☐	☐	☐	☐
	☐	☐	☐	☐
	☐	☐	☐	☐
	☐	☐	☐	☐
	☐	☐	☐	☐
	☐	☐	☐	☐
	☐	☐	☐	☐
	☐	☐	☐	☐

O – Ordered   R – Received
W – Wrapped   D – Delivered

Gift Tracker

Recipient Name	O	R	W	D
	☐	☐	☐	☐
	☐	☐	☐	☐
	☐	☐	☐	☐
	☐	☐	☐	☐
	☐	☐	☐	☐
	☐	☐	☐	☐
	☐	☐	☐	☐
	☐	☐	☐	☐
	☐	☐	☐	☐
	☐	☐	☐	☐
	☐	☐	☐	☐
	☐	☐	☐	☐

O – Ordered   R – Received
W – Wrapped   D – Delivered

Gift Tracker

Recipient Name	O	R	W	D
_____	☐	☐	☐	☐
_____	☐	☐	☐	☐
_____	☐	☐	☐	☐
_____	☐	☐	☐	☐
_____	☐	☐	☐	☐
_____	☐	☐	☐	☐
_____	☐	☐	☐	☐
_____	☐	☐	☐	☐
_____	☐	☐	☐	☐
_____	☐	☐	☐	☐
_____	☐	☐	☐	☐
_____	☐	☐	☐	☐

O – Ordered   R – Received
W – Wrapped   D – Delivered

Gift Tracker

Recipient Name	O	R	W	D
	☐	☐	☐	☐
	☐	☐	☐	☐
	☐	☐	☐	☐
	☐	☐	☐	☐
	☐	☐	☐	☐
	☐	☐	☐	☐
	☐	☐	☐	☐
	☐	☐	☐	☐
	☐	☐	☐	☐
	☐	☐	☐	☐
	☐	☐	☐	☐
	☐	☐	☐	☐

O – Ordered   R – Received
W – Wrapped   D – Delivered

Gift Tracker

Recipient Name	O	R	W	D
	☐	☐	☐	☐
	☐	☐	☐	☐
	☐	☐	☐	☐
	☐	☐	☐	☐
	☐	☐	☐	☐
	☐	☐	☐	☐
	☐	☐	☐	☐
	☐	☐	☐	☐
	☐	☐	☐	☐
	☐	☐	☐	☐
	☐	☐	☐	☐
	☐	☐	☐	☐

O – Ordered   R – Received
W – Wrapped   D – Delivered

Gift Tracker

Recipient Name	O	R	W	D
	☐	☐	☐	☐
	☐	☐	☐	☐
	☐	☐	☐	☐
	☐	☐	☐	☐
	☐	☐	☐	☐
	☐	☐	☐	☐
	☐	☐	☐	☐
	☐	☐	☐	☐
	☐	☐	☐	☐
	☐	☐	☐	☐
	☐	☐	☐	☐
	☐	☐	☐	☐

O – Ordered   R – Received
W – Wrapped   D – Delivered

Gift Tracker

Recipient Name	O	R	W	D
_____	☐	☐	☐	☐
_____	☐	☐	☐	☐
_____	☐	☐	☐	☐
_____	☐	☐	☐	☐
_____	☐	☐	☐	☐
_____	☐	☐	☐	☐
_____	☐	☐	☐	☐
_____	☐	☐	☐	☐
_____	☐	☐	☐	☐
_____	☐	☐	☐	☐
_____	☐	☐	☐	☐
_____	☐	☐	☐	☐

O – Ordered   R – Received
W – Wrapped   D – Delivered

Gift Tracker

Recipient Name	O	R	W	D
	☐	☐	☐	☐
	☐	☐	☐	☐
	☐	☐	☐	☐
	☐	☐	☐	☐
	☐	☐	☐	☐
	☐	☐	☐	☐
	☐	☐	☐	☐
	☐	☐	☐	☐
	☐	☐	☐	☐
	☐	☐	☐	☐
	☐	☐	☐	☐
	☐	☐	☐	☐

O – Ordered   R – Received
W – Wrapped   D – Delivered

Gift Tracker

Recipient Name	O	R	W	D
	☐	☐	☐	☐
	☐	☐	☐	☐
	☐	☐	☐	☐
	☐	☐	☐	☐
	☐	☐	☐	☐
	☐	☐	☐	☐
	☐	☐	☐	☐
	☐	☐	☐	☐
	☐	☐	☐	☐
	☐	☐	☐	☐
	☐	☐	☐	☐
	☐	☐	☐	☐

O – Ordered   R – Received
W – Wrapped   D – Delivered

My Family Gifts

Name –

Budget –

No.	Gift	Shop	O	R	W	Price
						Total

Stocking Stuffs

My Family Gifts

Name –

Budget –

No.	Gift	Shop	O	R	W	Price

Total

Stocking Stuffs

My Family Gifts

Name –

Budget –

No.	Gift	Shop	O	R	W	Price

Total

Stocking Stuffs

My Family Gifts

Name –

Budget –

No.	Gift	Shop	O	R	W	Price

Total

Stocking Stuffs

My Family Gifts

Name –

Budget –

No.	Gift	Shop	O	R	W	Price

Total

Stocking Stuffs

My Family Gifts

Name –

Budget –

No.	Gift	Shop	O	R	W	Price
					Total	

Stocking Stuffs

My Family Gifts

Name –

Budget –

No.	Gift	Shop	O	R	W	Price

Total

Stocking Stuffs

My Family Gifts

Name –

Budget –

No.	Gift	Shop	O	R	W	Price
						Total

Stocking Stuffs

 # My Family Gifts

Name –

Budget –

No.	Gift	Shop	O	R	W	Price
					Total	

Stocking Stuffs

 # My Family Gifts

Name –

Budget –

No.	Gift	Shop	O	R	W	Price

Total

Stocking Stuffs

My Family Gifts

Name –

Budget –

No.	Gift	Shop	O	R	W	Price
						Total

Stocking Stuffs

 # My Family Gifts

Name –

Budget –

No.	Gift	Shop	O	R	W	Price
					Total	

Stocking Stuffs

Christmas Decorations

Tree Decorations

Theme	Storage

What's in the Box

Decoration Box No. ⬭
_____
_____
_____
_____
_____
_____

Decoration Box No. ⬭
_____
_____
_____
_____
_____
_____

Decoration Box No. ⬭
_____
_____
_____
_____
_____
_____

Decoration Box No. ⬭
_____
_____
_____
_____
_____
_____

Decoration Box No. ⬭
_____
_____
_____
_____
_____
_____

Decoration Box No. ⬭
_____
_____
_____
_____
_____
_____

What's in the Box

Decoration Box No. ⬭

_____
_____
_____
_____
_____
_____

Decoration Box No. ⬭

_____
_____
_____
_____
_____
_____

Decoration Box No. ⬭

_____
_____
_____
_____
_____
_____

Decoration Box No. ⬭

_____
_____
_____
_____
_____
_____

Decoration Box No. ⬭

_____
_____
_____
_____
_____
_____

Decoration Box No. ⬭

_____
_____
_____
_____
_____
_____

What's in the Box

Decoration Box No. ▢
_____
_____
_____
_____
_____
_____

Decoration Box No. ▢
_____
_____
_____
_____
_____
_____

Decoration Box No. ▢
_____
_____
_____
_____
_____
_____
_____

Decoration Box No. ▢
_____
_____
_____
_____
_____
_____
_____

Decoration Box No. ▢
_____
_____
_____
_____
_____
_____
_____

Decoration Box No. ▢
_____
_____
_____
_____
_____
_____
_____

What's in the Box

Decoration Box No. ⬭
_____
_____
_____
_____
_____
_____
_____

Decoration Box No. ⬭
_____
_____
_____
_____
_____
_____
_____

Decoration Box No. ⬭
_____
_____
_____
_____
_____
_____
_____

Decoration Box No. ⬭
_____
_____
_____
_____
_____
_____
_____

Decoration Box No. ⬭
_____
_____
_____
_____
_____
_____

Decoration Box No. ⬭
_____
_____
_____
_____
_____
_____

What's in the Box

Decoration Box No. ⬭

Decoration Box No. ⬭

Decoration Box No. ⬭

Decoration Box No. ⬭

Decoration Box No. ⬭

Decoration Box No. ⬭

What's in the Box

Decoration Box No. ☐

_____
_____
_____
_____
_____
_____
_____

Decoration Box No. ☐

_____
_____
_____
_____
_____
_____
_____

Decoration Box No. ☐

_____
_____
_____
_____
_____
_____
_____

Decoration Box No. ☐

_____
_____
_____
_____
_____
_____
_____

Decoration Box No. ☐

_____
_____
_____
_____
_____
_____
_____

Decoration Box No. ☐

_____
_____
_____
_____
_____
_____
_____

Decor Inventory

Location

Theme	Storage

Location

Theme	Storage

Location

Theme	Storage

Location

Theme	Storage

Decor Inventory

Theme	Storage

Location

Theme	Storage

Location

Theme	Storage

Location

Theme	Storage

Decor Inventory

Location

Theme	Storage

Location

Theme	Storage

Location

Theme	Storage

Location

Theme	Storage

Decor Inventory

Location

Theme	Storage

Location

Theme	Storage

Location

Theme	Storage

Location

Theme	Storage

 # Recipe Ideas

Recipe Name: _____ Serves: Prep Time: Cook Time:

Ingredients: Directions:

Recipe Name: _____ Serves: Prep Time: Cook Time:

Ingredients: Directions:

Recipe Name: _____ Serves: Prep Time: Cook Time:

Ingredients: Directions:

Recipe Ideas

Recipe Name: _____ Serves: Prep Time: Cook Time:
Ingredients: Directions:

Recipe Name: _____ Serves: Prep Time: Cook Time:
Ingredients: Directions:

Recipe Name: _____ Serves: Prep Time: Cook Time:
Ingredients: Directions:

 # Recipe Ideas

Recipe Name: _____ Serves: Prep Time: Cook Time:

Ingredients: Directions:

Recipe Name: _____ Serves: Prep Time: Cook Time:

Ingredients: Directions:

Recipe Name: _____ Serves: Prep Time: Cook Time:

Ingredients: Directions:

Recipe Ideas

Recipe Name: _____ Serves: Prep Time: Cook Time:

Ingredients: Directions:

Recipe Name: _____ Serves: Prep Time: Cook Time:

Ingredients: Directions:

Recipe Name: _____ Serves: Prep Time: Cook Time:

Ingredients: Directions:

 # Recipe Ideas

Recipe Name: _____   Serves: Prep Time: Cook Time:

Ingredients: Directions:

Recipe Name: _____   Serves: Prep Time: Cook Time:

Ingredients: Directions:

Recipe Name: _____   Serves: Prep Time: Cook Time:

Ingredients: Directions:

Recipe Ideas

Recipe Name: _____ Serves: Prep Time: Cook Time:

Ingredients: Directions:

Recipe Name: _____ Serves: Prep Time: Cook Time:

Ingredients: Directions:

Recipe Name: _____ Serves: Prep Time: Cook Time:

Ingredients: Directions:

 # Recipe Ideas

Recipe Name: _____ Serves: Prep Time: Cook Time:

Ingredients: Directions:

Recipe Name: _____ Serves: Prep Time: Cook Time:

Ingredients: Directions:

Recipe Name: _____ Serves: Prep Time: Cook Time:

Ingredients: Directions:

Recipe Ideas

Recipe Name: _____ Serves: Prep Time: Cook Time:

Ingredients: Directions:

Recipe Name: _____ Serves: Prep Time: Cook Time:

Ingredients: Directions:

Recipe Name: _____ Serves: Prep Time: Cook Time:

Ingredients: Directions:

 # Recipe Ideas

Recipe Name: _____   Serves: Prep Time: Cook Time:

Ingredients: Directions:

Recipe Name: _____   Serves: Prep Time: Cook Time:

Ingredients: Directions:

Recipe Name: _____   Serves: Prep Time: Cook Time:

Ingredients: Directions:

Recipe Ideas

Recipe Name: _____   Serves: Prep Time: Cook Time:

Ingredients: Directions:

Recipe Name: _____   Serves: Prep Time: Cook Time:

Ingredients: Directions:

Recipe Name: _____   Serves: Prep Time: Cook Time:

Ingredients: Directions:

 # Recipe Ideas

Recipe Name: _____   Serves: Prep Time: Cook Time:

Ingredients: Directions:

Recipe Name: _____   Serves: Prep Time: Cook Time:

Ingredients: Directions:

Recipe Name: _____   Serves: Prep Time: Cook Time:

Ingredients: Directions:

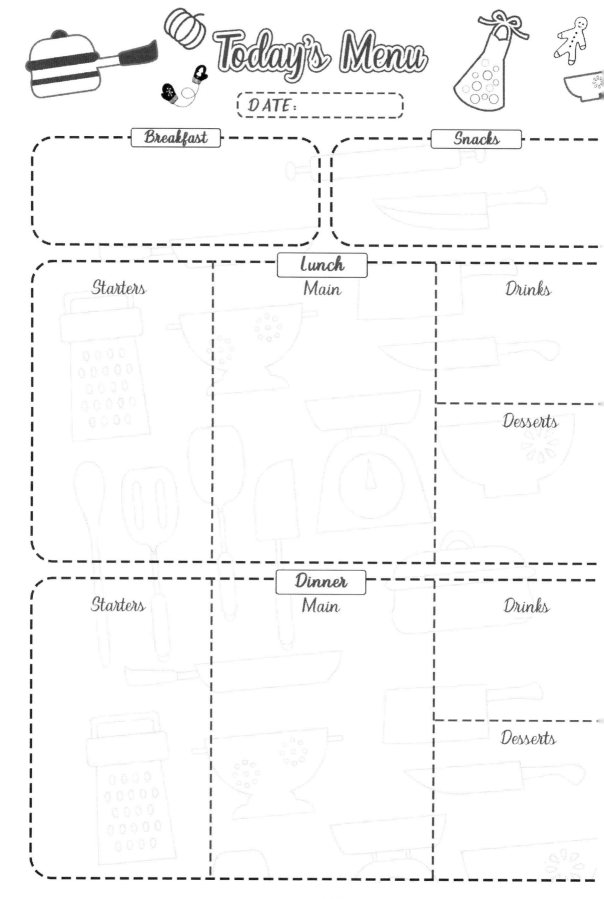

Today's Menu

DATE:

Breakfast

Snacks

Lunch

Starters

Main

Drinks

Desserts

Dinner

Starters

Main

Drinks

Desserts

Food Shopping List

Notes:

Cooking Preparation

Dish	Cooking time	B	P	C
		☐	☐	☐
		☐	☐	☐
		☐	☐	☐
		☐	☐	☐
		☐	☐	☐
		☐	☐	☐
		☐	☐	☐
		☐	☐	☐
		☐	☐	☐
		☐	☐	☐
		☐	☐	☐
		☐	☐	☐
		☐	☐	☐
		☐	☐	☐
		☐	☐	☐
		☐	☐	☐
		☐	☐	☐
		☐	☐	☐

B – Bought   P – Prepped   C – Cooked

Cooking Schedule

Time		
6.00a.m		☐
6.30a.m		☐
7.00a.m		☐
7.30a.m		☐
8.00a.m		☐
8.30a.m		☐
9.00a.m		☐
9.30a.m		☐
0.00a.m		☐
0.30a.m		☐
11.00a.m		☐
12.00a.m		☐
12.30a.m		☐
1.00p.m		☐
2.00p.m		☐
3.00p.m		☐
4.00p.m		☐
5.00p.m		☐
6.00p.m		☐
7.00p.m		☐
7.30p.m		☐
8.00p.m		☐
8.30p.m		☐
9.00p.m		☐

Today's Menu

DATE:

Breakfast

Snacks

Lunch

Starters

Main

Drinks

Desserts

Dinner

Starters

Main

Drinks

Desserts

Food Shopping List

Notes:

Cooking Preparation

Dish	Cooking time	B	P	C

B – Bought   P – Prepped   C – Cooked

Cooking Schedule

Time		
6.00a.m		☐
6.30a.m		☐
7.00a.m		☐
7.30a.m		☐
8.00a.m		☐
8.30a.m		☐
9.00a.m		☐
9.30a.m		☐
0.00a.m		☐
10.30a.m		☐
11.00a.m		☐
12.00a.m		☐
12.30a.m		☐
1.00p.m		☐
2.00p.m		☐
3.00p.m		☐
4.00p.m		☐
5.00p.m		☐
6.00p.m		☐
7.00p.m		☐
7.30p.m		☐
8.00p.m		☐
8.30p.m		☐
9.00p.m		☐

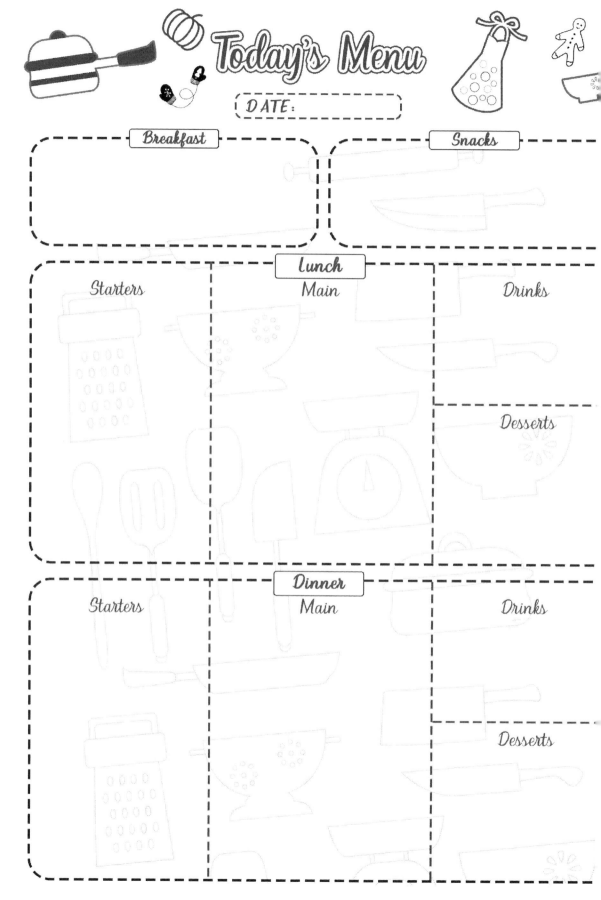

Today's Menu

DATE:

Breakfast

Snacks

Lunch

Starters

Main

Drinks

Desserts

Dinner

Starters

Main

Drinks

Desserts

Food Shopping List

Notes:

Cooking Preparation

Dish	Cooking time	B	P	C
		☐	☐	☐
		☐	☐	☐
		☐	☐	☐
		☐	☐	☐
		☐	☐	☐
		☐	☐	☐
		☐	☐	☐
		☐	☐	☐
		☐	☐	☐
		☐	☐	☐
		☐	☐	☐
		☐	☐	☐
		☐	☐	☐
		☐	☐	☐
		☐	☐	☐
		☐	☐	☐
		☐	☐	☐
		☐	☐	☐

B – Bought   P – Prepped   C – Cooked

Cooking Schedule

Time	
6.00a.m	
6.30a.m	
7.00a.m	
7.30a.m	
8.00a.m	
8.30a.m	
9.00a.m	
9.30a.m	
0.00a.m	
10.30a.m	
11.00a.m	
12.00a.m	
12.30a.m	
1.00p.m	
2.00p.m	
3.00p.m	
4.00p.m	
5.00p.m	
6.00p.m	
7.00p.m	
7.30p.m	
8.00p.m	
8.30p.m	
9.00p.m	

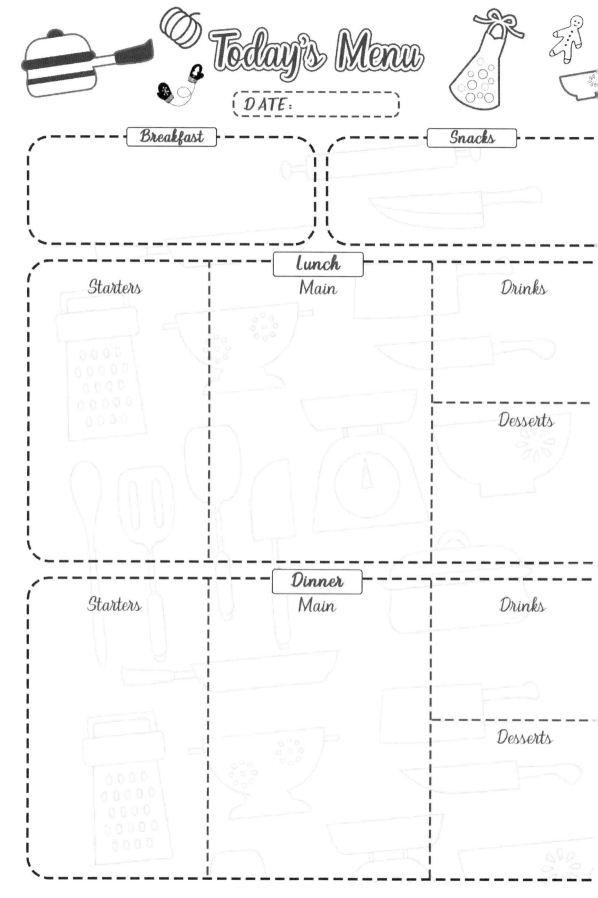

Today's Menu

DATE:

Breakfast

Snacks

Lunch

Starters

Main

Drinks

Desserts

Dinner

Starters

Main

Drinks

Desserts

Food Shopping List

Notes:

Cooking Preparation

Dish	Cooking time	B	P	C
		☐	☐	☐
		☐	☐	☐
		☐	☐	☐
		☐	☐	☐
		☐	☐	☐
		☐	☐	☐
		☐	☐	☐
		☐	☐	☐
		☐	☐	☐
		☐	☐	☐
		☐	☐	☐
		☐	☐	☐
		☐	☐	☐
		☐	☐	☐
		☐	☐	☐
		☐	☐	☐
		☐	☐	☐
		☐	☐	☐

B – Bought   P – Prepped   C – Cooked

Cooking Schedule

Time	
6.00a.m	
6.30a.m	
7.00a.m	
7.30a.m	
8.00a.m	
8.30a.m	
9.00a.m	
9.30a.m	
0.00a.m	
10.30a.m	
11.00a.m	
12.00a.m	
12.30a.m	
1.00p.m	
2.00p.m	
3.00p.m	
4.00p.m	
5.00p.m	
6.00p.m	
7.00p.m	
7.30p.m	
8.00p.m	
8.30p.m	
9.00p.m	

Today's Menu

DATE:

Breakfast

Snacks

Lunch

Starters

Main

Drinks

Desserts

Dinner

Starters

Main

Drinks

Desserts

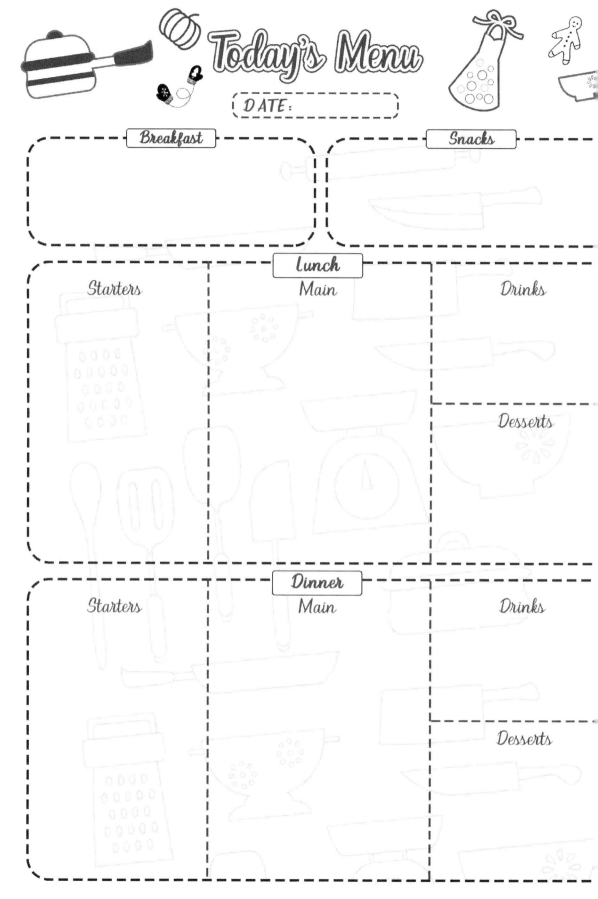

Food Shopping List

Notes:

Cooking Preparation

Dish	Cooking time	B	P	C
		☐	☐	☐
		☐	☐	☐
		☐	☐	☐
		☐	☐	☐
		☐	☐	☐
		☐	☐	☐
		☐	☐	☐
		☐	☐	☐
		☐	☐	☐
		☐	☐	☐
		☐	☐	☐
		☐	☐	☐
		☐	☐	☐
		☐	☐	☐
		☐	☐	☐
		☐	☐	☐
		☐	☐	☐
		☐	☐	☐

B – Bought   P – Prepped   C – Cooked

Cooking Schedule

Time	
6.00a.m	☐
6.30a.m	☐
7.00a.m	☐
7.30a.m	☐
8.00a.m	☐
8.30a.m	☐
9.00a.m	☐
9.30a.m	☐
0.00a.m	☐
10.30a.m	☐
11.00a.m	☐
12.00a.m	☐
12.30a.m	☐
1.00p.m	☐
2.00p.m	☐
3.00p.m	☐
4.00p.m	☐
5.00p.m	☐
6.00p.m	☐
7.00p.m	☐
7.30p.m	☐
8.00p.m	☐
8.30p.m	☐
9.00p.m	☐

Today's Menu

DATE:

Breakfast

Snacks

Lunch

Starters

Main

Drinks

Desserts

Dinner

Starters

Main

Drinks

Desserts

Food Shopping List

Notes:

Cooking Preparation

Dish	Cooking time	B	P	C
		☐	☐	☐
		☐	☐	☐
		☐	☐	☐
		☐	☐	☐
		☐	☐	☐
		☐	☐	☐
		☐	☐	☐
		☐	☐	☐
		☐	☐	☐
		☐	☐	☐
		☐	☐	☐
		☐	☐	☐
		☐	☐	☐
		☐	☐	☐
		☐	☐	☐
		☐	☐	☐
		☐	☐	☐
		☐	☐	☐

B – Bought   P – Prepped   C – Cooked

Cooking Schedule

Time		
6.00a.m		☐
6.30a.m		☐
7.00a.m		☐
7.30a.m		☐
8.00a.m		☐
8.30a.m		☐
9.00a.m		☐
9.30a.m		☐
0.00a.m		☐
10.30a.m		☐
11.00a.m		☐
12.00a.m		☐
12.30a.m		☐
1.00p.m		☐
2.00p.m		☐
3.00p.m		☐
4.00p.m		☐
5.00p.m		☐
6.00p.m		☐
7.00p.m		☐
7.30p.m		☐
8.00p.m		☐
8.30p.m		☐
9.00p.m		☐

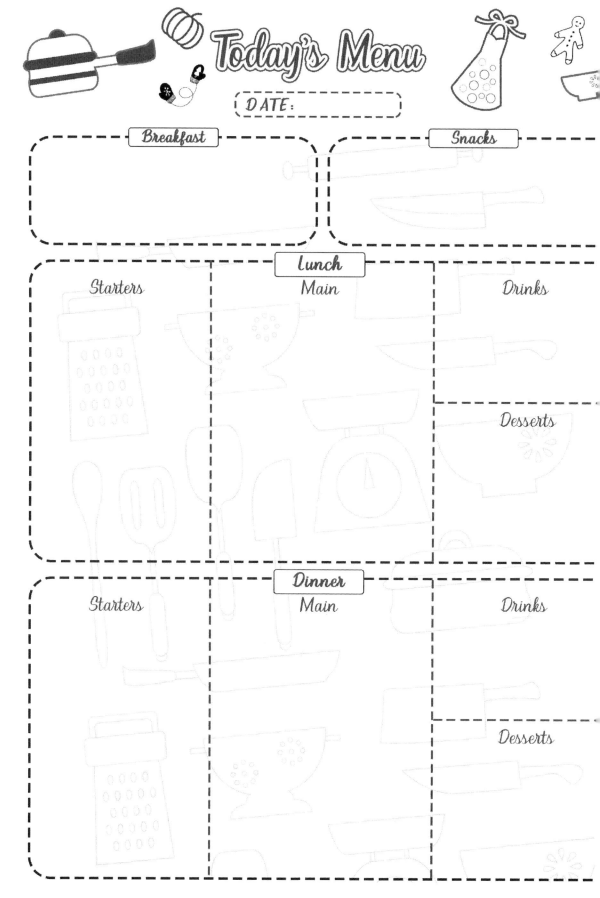

Today's Menu

DATE:

Breakfast

Snacks

Lunch

Starters

Main

Drinks

Desserts

Dinner

Starters

Main

Drinks

Desserts

Food Shopping List

Notes:

Cooking Preparation

Dish	Cooking time	B	P	C
		☐	☐	☐
		☐	☐	☐
		☐	☐	☐
		☐	☐	☐
		☐	☐	☐
		☐	☐	☐
		☐	☐	☐
		☐	☐	☐
		☐	☐	☐
		☐	☐	☐
		☐	☐	☐
		☐	☐	☐
		☐	☐	☐
		☐	☐	☐
		☐	☐	☐
		☐	☐	☐

B – Bought   P – Prepped   C – Cooked

Cooking Schedule

Time	
6.00a.m	
6.30a.m	
7.00a.m	
7.30a.m	
8.00a.m	
8.30a.m	
9.00a.m	
9.30a.m	
0.00a.m	
0.30a.m	
11.00a.m	
12.00a.m	
12.30a.m	
1.00p.m	
2.00p.m	
3.00p.m	
4.00p.m	
5.00p.m	
6.00p.m	
7.00p.m	
7.30p.m	
8.00p.m	
8.30p.m	
9.00p.m	

Festive Shopping List

Festive Shopping List

Festive Shopping List

Festive Shopping List

Festive Shopping List

Festive Shopping List

Festive Shopping List

Festive Shopping List

Deal Comparision

Item :

Stores	Description	Price

Item :

Stores	Description	Price

Item :

Stores	Description	Price

Deal Comparision

Item :

Stores	Description	Price

Item :

Stores	Description	Price

Item :

Stores	Description	Price

Deal Comparision

Item :

Stores	Description	Price

Item :

Stores	Description	Price

Item :

Stores	Description	Price

Deal Comparision

Item :

Stores	Description	Price

Item :

Stores	Description	Price

Item :

Stores	Description	Price

Deal Comparision

Item :

Stores	Description	Price

Item :

Stores	Description	Price

Item :

Stores	Description	Price

Deal Comparision

Item :

Stores	Description	Price

Item :

Stores	Description	Price

Item :

Stores	Description	Price

Deal Comparision

Item :

Stores	Description	Price

Item :

Stores	Description	Price

Item :

Stores	Description	Price

Deal Comparision

Item :

Stores	Description	Price

Item :

Stores	Description	Price

Item :

Stores	Description	Price

Deal Comparision

Item :

Stores	Description	Price

Item :

Stores	Description	Price

Item :

Stores	Description	Price

Deal Comparision

Item :

Stores	Description	Price

Item :

Stores	Description	Price

Item :

Stores	Description	Price

Deal Comparision

Item :

Stores	Description	Price

Item :

Stores	Description	Price

Item :

Stores	Description	Price

Deal Comparision

Item :

Stores	Description	Price

Item :

Stores	Description	Price

Item :

Stores	Description	Price

Deal Comparision

Item :

Stores	Description	Price

Item :

Stores	Description	Price

Item :

Stores	Description	Price

Deal Comparision

Item :

Stores	Description	Price

Item :

Stores	Description	Price

Item :

Stores	Description	Price

Deal Comparision

Item :

Stores	Description	Price

Item :

Stores	Description	Price

Item :

Stores	Description	Price

Deal Comparision

Item :

Stores	Description	Price

Item :

Stores	Description	Price

Item :

Stores	Description	Price

Deal Comparision

Item :

Stores	Description	Price

Item :

Stores	Description	Price

Item :

Stores	Description	Price

Expense Tracker

Stores	Description	Price	Stores	Description	Price
				Running total	
	Total			Total	

Expense Tracker

Stores	Description	Price	Stores	Description	Price
	Running total			Running total	
	Total			Total	

Expense Tracker

Stores	Description	Price
	Running total	
	Total	

Stores	Description	Price
	Running total	
	Total	

Expense Tracker

Stores	Description	Price		Stores	Description	Price
	Running total				Running total	
	Total				Total	

Expense Tracker

Stores	Description	Price
	Running total	
	Total	

Stores	Description	Price
	Running total	
	Total	

Expense Tracker

Stores	Description	Price	Stores	Description	Price
	Running total			Running total	
	Total			Total	

Expense Tracker

Stores	Description	Price
	Running total	
	Total	

Stores	Description	Price
	Running total	
	Total	

Expense Tracker

Stores	Description	Price	Stores	Description	Price
	Running total			Running total	
	Total			Grand Total	

My Scribbles

My Scribbles

My Scribbles

My Scribbles

My Scribbles

Notes for Next Year

Notes for Next Year

Notes for Next Year

Notes for Next Year

Printed in Great Britain
by Amazon